# Embrace ME the Real ME

## CHERYL LYNNE

# Embrace Me, The Real Me

By: Cheryl Lynne

Embrace Me: The Real Me

Copyright © 2024 by Cheryl Lynne

Published by Grace 4 Purpose, Publishing Co. LLC

All rights reserved. No part of this publication may be reproduced in any form or by any electronic or mechanical means, including information storage and retrieval systems, without prior permission in writing from the publisher, except by reviewers, who may quote brief passages in a review.

All scripture quotations, unless otherwise indicated, are taken from the King James Version of the Bible, unless otherwise indicated. All rights reserved.

ISBN: 979-8-9908003-9-7

Editing by: Grace 4 Purpose, Publishing Co. LLC

Book cover design by Grace 4 Purpose, Publishing Co. LLC

Author Photo Credit: Photo by Cherise'

Printed and bound in the United States of America

# Dedication

To my partner Aaron, thanks for telling me not to quit, encouraging me when I didn't know where to start, and loving me the whole package.

To my children Kayla, Destini, John, Leon, Bobby, and Biana, thank you for your *"wuv,"* support, and patience during those long days and nights. Never stop dreaming.

To my SPHS Step Team family Joe, Karon and Wanda thanks for the support and the ear to listen to me venting or reading a chapter again and again, telling me to just do it.

# Table of Contents

**Introduction**

**Phase One: The Beginning**

**Phase Two: Be Open to the Process**

**Phase Three: Position Your Heart and Real Digging**

**Phase Four: Embracing Yourself**

**Phase Five: Don't Be Scared! Walk forward and rebirth**

*Our deepest fear is not that we are inadequate,*
*Our deepest fear is that we are Powerful beyond measure.*
*We ask ourselves, 'Who am I to be brilliant,*
*Gorgeous, talented, fabulous?'*
*We were born to make manifest the glory of God that is within us.*
*And as we let our own light shine.*
*We give other people permission to do the same.*
*-Marianne Williamson*

---

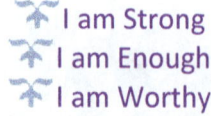

🕊 I am Strong
🕊 I am Enough
🕊 I am Worthy

# Introduction

One of the most difficult questions to answer is: Who are you? Tell me about yourself? Not the typical biography; honestly, answering these questions requires you to quiet yourself and strip away layers. Are you constantly worried about what others think of you? When you must face your fears alone, don't be a slave to others' opinions about you. Instead, take back control and understand yourself when no one else does or believes in you. Stand TALL.

We all experience ups and downs. John 10:10 says, "The thief's purpose is to steal and kill and destroy. My PURPOSE is to give them a rich and satisfying life." This encompasses all areas of life: spiritual, mental, physical, emotional, financial, and social. This is self-love, self-worth, and self-care. In an era where we forget our worth, be your authentic self without worrying about others' perceptions—without the makeup, wigs, or clothes. Be honest with yourself; sometimes, we have doubts, fears, or just don't know. We often neglect self-love. So, who are you? Who are you when you close your front door and are all by yourself? Who are you when you look at yourself in the mirror?

---

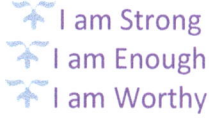

🕊 I am Strong
🕊 I am Enough
🕊 I am Worthy

Get ready to journal or take notes because we're about to unpack and uncover the real you. In this journey, I had to tell my truth. I sought, searched, and hid to find ME. I am grateful I didn't stop; I paid my tolls, kept going, and left it on that road. I didn't just change my mindset; I reset my mind, eyes, ears, heart, and soul, focusing on my heavenly father. I am FREE. This is my truth of overcoming and EMBRACING THE TOTAL ME.

---

🕊 I am Strong
🕊 I am Enough
🕊 I am Worthy

# PHASE ONE: THE BEGINNING

It took a long time for me to reach this place of embracing all of me and loving every inch of my body—inside and out; acknowledging the good, the bad, and the indifferent. Yes, it took years because I had to be completely honest with myself. I had to be open and vulnerable and allow myself to be uncomfortable; I even had to rename myself. In essence, I had to embrace the process and tap into my inner strength—a battle akin to Ali vs. Joe—the old Cheryl vs. Purpose Cheryl. This meant I had to combat my old ways, my trauma, my triggers, and my past to let the purposeful Cheryl emerge. It might sound strange or crazy, but at birth, we were honored with three names: first, middle, and last.

My name is Cheryl Lynne Miller. Let me break it down. Cheryl's origin is Spanish, Welsh, American, Christian, English, French, and German roots. It means dependable, but in Welsh, it signifies various forms of love. Lynn can be a unisex name with origins in Anglo, Australian, and French, where it means waterfall and cascade. In French, it connects to Tennyson's story of Sir Gareth and Lynette. Miller, with origins in Australian and Latin, means one who grinds grain.

---

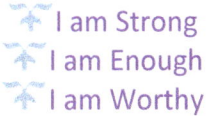

✦ I am Strong
✦ I am Enough
✦ I am Worthy

My birth name is our first handle; I had to find her first. As we grow older, we can use our names to fit different situations. For example, there could be three Linda Alice Jacksons in your business or school. One will use Linda Jackson, another will use their middle name (Linda A. Jackson), and the last person will use the letter L and the last name (L. Jackson). They all share the name Linda Alice Jackson but use it differently.

The old Cheryl was lost and confused from the moment I was born. I had problems and labels already attached to me before I entered the world. I say this because my mother and father were going through their own challenges when I was in the womb. I believe that if parents are broken spiritually, that unborn child might feel that energy, if not initially. I realized that my household's culture was different from everyone else's. For example, if your family talks very loudly at home, which mine does, if I come to your household, you might think I'm yelling. I had to reset my mindset. Similarly, if the family doesn't say 'Thank you' or 'Please,' we might perceive it as disrespectful.

By the time I was a teenager, numerous life events had happened to me. I lost my father at the age of eight, and my mother and siblings were doing their own things—drugs, marriages, having children, and working; doing things that a child should not see. Some

---

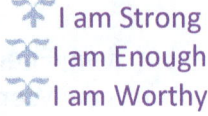

🕊 I am Strong
🕊 I am Enough
🕊 I am Worthy

family members put labels on me because of their own guilt or shame. Life events as a child can mold you and shape how you treat yourself and see things as an adult. For me, it was molestation, rape, being beaten, abandoned, homeless, becoming a stripper, the list goes on. But I made it through it all.

When I was around eight or maybe nine, the house we lived in was very cold to me with people constantly coming in and out. My family at the time celebrated everything – new jobs, losing jobs, moving, birthdays, breakups, or just chilling. We often played cards with my mother's friends, and my siblings' friends would come over too. I can remember a time when there was a bar across the street, and on Friday and Saturday nights, they wouldn't play the music box. Instead, they'd open the bar doors and ask my mother to put the speakers in the windows because she played better music.

My mother did her best raising us with what she had. I can say she gave her best at that time. She poured into us education, love, morals, and values. However, since she was in the midst of her own storms, things slipped by her. One weekend night, the house was alive with music, people playing spades or pinnacles and drinking and smoking. I was a scrawny, lanky girl with very dark skin who could barely speak. I wore big white Coca-Cola glasses that didn't fit my face

---

properly, making my skin feel tough and look like elephant skin. Growing up, I had never felt more invisible.

This grown man was so drunk and high I could smell the vodka and the weed all over him when he came into my room. He startled me out of my sleep and woke me up. He was touching and fondling me, so I started to fight him. His hands were too strong, and I yelled, but the music and talking drowned my voice. He said to me, "No one cares, and you are doing me a favor because your sibling won't put out." That was the first of many days. When he came around, I thought I was safe if I pretended to be sleeping downstairs on the couch, but that didn't work for long. So happy he didn't last long.

We were constantly moving, struggling to strive, and I really didn't have a structured life. When I became an adult, I found myself moving every five minutes too. This was my normal until I realized it and wanted to change it. I tried to become an adult fast due to life events. I held onto words that people said, trusting too easily. The very people that were supposed to support and love me, adult family members, were the ones that destroyed me. By the time I reached high school, I was an awkward, broken butterfly trying to fit in where it didn't seem to fit. Around this time, I was called ugly so much that it became embedded in me. To me, the word "ugly" meant unimportant, unseen,

---

🕊 I am Strong
🕊 I am Enough
🕊 I am Worthy

unheard, that people didn't care to understand me. This feeling carried me well past high school and into my adult years.

Where I lived, everyone knew everybody, so I got bullied for the way I talked, the way I dressed, my family situations, and my appearance. I lied so much because I didn't want to get jumped or picked on due to some people knowing that my siblings and mother were on drugs. I lied, tried selling drugs, and in my late adult life, became a stripper. When your own family says you're less than because of your last name, it hurts. My grandmother never liked or cared for my father, which I can understand because of his trials and tribulations. He was very abusive to my mother, and though I have memories of that, the impact didn't fully surface until I was in therapy, working on something else.

My grandmother told me that it was "Washington, Perkins, then Miller" for so long that my cousins started saying it. I laughed, thinking it was funny, but then I realized I was the only Miller in the family. They were telling me that, in their eyes, Miller is less than them, that my children and their children will be less than. I couldn't let this be. I had to find out who Cheryl was in the world. Thanks to my mother and godmother, who instilled in me that I am loved and played songs to me, a seed was planted. I didn't know

---

✦ I am Strong
✦ I am Enough
✦ I am Worthy

adventurous. I told them that the "old Cheryl" was depressed and lonely, did stupid things, and made reckless decisions that almost cost me my life. I had to grow up too early and saw a lot in my early years. Some family members treated me differently because of my parents' actions, and some things I did were stupid. For example, I believed every male who said he loved me and that we were in a relationship, only to find out I was lied to—I was not in a relationship with those males. I saw them when it was convenient for them.

    I could not connect with my peers; I felt like an outsider, sometimes scared to speak because I thought no one could understand me, or they would make fun of me. Everyone was doing their own thing, and I was screaming for help. People were hurting me verbally, mentally, and physically, and no one saw it. I was so alone that I made an imaginary friend up until I was eleven. Her name was AB. Some older family members told me that I was nothing because of who my father was; they said I won't be anything because of my speech—I can't go to college; I was curved. This family member said, "You're probably better off on your back; you don't have anything for yourself." It was weird; this person was supposed to love me unconditionally, but they pulled me down. As a young teenager, she put labels on me that I wore for a long time. If you hear this day in and day out, you will eventually stop fighting.

---

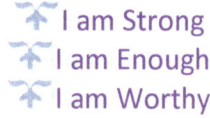
🕊 I am Strong
🕊 I am Enough
🕊 I am Worthy

I had to embrace uncertainty trauma and empower myself to take risks. Only two people know that I was so depressed in middle school that I started to self-harm. My self-esteem was so low; it was -8. Yes, I had priceless moments here and there in my years, but every now and then, something or someone put me in that dark space again. At this time, I was getting bullied about my image and my voice. One of the homes I lived in was so bad that when it rained, the walls got wet. In one of the bedrooms, there was a hole in the ceiling, and every other month there was no heat. Kerosene was in my clothes; we had to layer up when we went to bed. I borrowed my older sibling's clothes, but if you asked her, I was stealing them. Back then, I couldn't afford Reebok or Nike; it was all I could afford. Yes, I waited for my sister to take my nieces and nephews to school so I could wear the outfit she wore the day before. When I came home, I tried to put it back before she went to bed. Sometimes, I had to pay to borrow her stuff; it was not cheap.

I started avoiding my problems so much that, as an adult, it turned into running away from my problems. Until I could not run anymore, I had to face everything. When you go through something like this, it's like being sick. You don't know when you have to go to the bathroom, but you know it's coming. You're uncertain about what end it will come out of, how much will come out, or when it will happen. So, what I'm

---

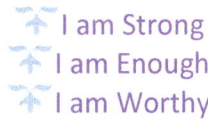
🕊 I am Strong
🕊 I am Enough
🕊 I am Worthy

saying is, when you finally stand still and want to change your mindset, everything you've been through will come out in different forms—depression, behavioral issues, silence. I don't want to put a Band-Aid on something that needs an operation. I've learned that if you run away from a problem or situation, you will have to deal with it sooner or later, and later is much harder than sooner.

I'm giving you a snapshot of my life. The funny thing is that my character never changed. I was hurt, confused about the situation, and thought it was my fault. I yearned to belong to this family member so much that I took their hurt and put it on myself. I came to the conclusion that the only person I can control is me. I don't want people to pick on me. I want to change that image of me because it was a doormat, less than worthless. I had to find myself, and she was buried so deep in piles of gravel that I had to excavate, shovel, and claw my way out. When I started, I didn't know what I was starting and what I would find... ME.

---

🕊 I am Strong
🕊 I am Enough
🕊 I am Worthy

**Exercise One:**
Write three/ four sentences about who are you?

_____

_____

_____

_____

✈ I am Strong
✈ I am Enough
✈ I am Worthy

# PHASE TWO

### Be Open to the Process

In 2009, I tried to end my life when my health started to decline because no one believed in me. My migraines were excruciating, and doctors suspected a brain tumor. My head felt like fifty 18-wheelers were driving back and forth on it, with about 100,000 straight pins poking my eyes and forehead. I lost my house, working 40 hours in one weekend and part-time 15-20 hours on weekdays. My marriage was failing because, deep down, I knew he was cheating, but I felt I deserved it. I had a child who needed a father. He was a good father, but a bad husband. So, I had to rebuild my fence. At that time, my fence was so low that it was flat below ground. I had to build it high enough so people wouldn't want to climb it, reclaim my respect and confidence, and conquer fear and doubt. Let me tell you, fear and doubt followed me, and I tried my hardest to shake them until I surrendered to God.

Now, remember, my mother was many things, but we went to church, and the school we attended was a Catholic school, so we had 55 minutes of religion and one hour of church on Sundays. Religion was introduced to me as a young child. I didn't know the power of prayer. I can say that since I was not much of a talker or reader, we were a music family. I would

---

🕊 I am Strong
🕊 I am Enough
🕊 I am Worthy

listen to BeBe and CeCe Winans, Shirley Caesar, Andre Crouch, and Oldies but Goodies like, The Temptations, Earth Wind and Fire, and The Jackson 5. That music pulled me through, but after a while, it did not sustain me.

    I recall my aunt and uncle would come around and ask every Sunday if I was going to church. I'd say nope, and they'd say okay, they'd be back next Sunday. This went on for about six to eight months. One beautiful sunny Sunday morning, my aunt and uncle had just left my house. I called my girlfriend, and she wanted to go to the gallery. I told her I'd meet her at her house. As I strolled my way to her house, I heard an angelic sound. It was breathtaking, and I found peace in this sound, not knowing where this phenomenal, spectacular sound was coming from. As I got close to the building, it was a church. I had to see who was singing. When I opened the door and adjusted my focus because tears were rolling down my eyes, I was unexpectedly flabbergasted by who I saw. My aunt had this sensational voice that put a chill on me. She noticed me, her hands opened for me, and I sprinted, maybe leapt, into her arms. I didn't want to let her go. Now, remember, I said I was a Catholic. I was in a space of the unknown, and all I remember is going down (like Joe Frazier when he went down). I don't remember what happened. My aunt said I was on the floor almost until the end of the service. My aunt went

---

🕊️ I am Strong
🕊️ I am Enough
🕊️ I am Worthy

to a Baptist church. Now, I am not that person; I was reborn again. I am still Cheryl, but a different verse. If someone asks you at this very moment, "Who are you?" what will you say?

In the Bible, God used Abram and Sarai to become Abraham and Sarah, Jacob to become Israel, and Simon to become Peter. For them to walk in purpose, God had to change their names (rebirth). Same people, different mindset. Remember, I said at the beginning your name means something, and we can use it how it fits. When we are born or get older, family and friends start putting labels on us, some good and some bad. "She's mean," "He's stupid," "She's so smart," "He'll be the first in the family to make it," and the list goes on. We must rebuild ourselves in a way that removes the negative and puts three letters, two words in front of everything. These two words are powerful: "I am." But we are afraid of one word, two letters. Why? The word is "no."

I was born with a speech impediment, I also had dark skin and that wasn't popular in the '80s. I had bad eczema between the ages of six and twenty. Some family members denied me because of who my father/mother was or what they were doing. Yes, I had siblings, but I felt alone at times, maybe because we were not close in age. They did not relate to me growing up, and I did not relate to them. They were

---

✝ I am Strong
✝ I am Enough
✝ I am Worthy

dealing with parents, marriages, or just life. For years, family members imposed their thoughts on me. I was young and didn't understand the process of what they were doing. Sometimes, it was funny, but day in and day out, it took a toll on me. Your peers in school or the community see you differently because you don't want to follow them. You know inside you don't want to do this, but you want to fit in, and you're not like them. It's strange; we were brought up to be ourselves, taught to be different because everyone else is already taken. The moment you try to be yourself, someone asks why you dress like that, why you do that, why you act like this, or why you want to be that. You just say, "I'm finding myself, being myself. I'm trying." And now they say it's wrong to do this because they see you doing something else. I'm confused now.

  I was a people-pleaser, always wanting to make everyone happy, but I wasn't happy myself. I did this for years. In 2008, I started the process while I was still on my journey. I can say I stopped and started again, making it a long process, but after my last loved one died in 2018, I knew it was time to have a backbone. Throughout those years, I was preparing. God will give you a vision or a saying, but it's not always time to reveal it. I was in training for my next fight, me vs. me—the rebirth of Cheryl. I had to find my voice quickly, and to do that, I had to surrender everything to God (James 4:10 - "Humble yourselves before the

---

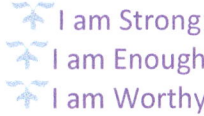

Lord, and he will exalt you"). I knew of God, but I didn't really know Him. I had to give everything to Him, even the 0.02% that I wasn't doing right. Songs like "I Surrender All to You" by William McDowell and "Yes" by Shekinah Glory became my anthems. Listening to them, I found encouragement within myself, echoing the sentiments of Donald Lawrence.

    I allowed people to impose their thoughts and fears onto me, unaware of the negative effects it had. If someone told me, "Why are you doing that? That sounds crazy," or my favorite, "Don't do that; I don't think you can do that," I realized people had stolen many ideas, and others got credit for my own. Finally, I understood that they wanted me to be silent—they saw something in me that I hadn't seen yet. I am a strong, intelligent Black woman with a creative mind. I learned to use "RE": renew my mindset, recharge my energy, refound my path, rebuild my village, and let go of some things and some people in my life, and reset my goals. I had to use my silence as power, remembering the old saying, "Don't let your left hand know what the right hand is doing." I used to be so excited to let everyone in on my plans, but some people killed the dream before it could grow. I became so accustomed to silence that when I tried to use my voice, it got lost.

    At this stage, I learned to "Be stronger than your fears and bigger than your insecurities." I started to

---

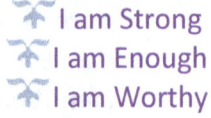

    🕊 I am Strong
    🕊 I am Enough
    🕊 I am Worthy

own my flaws and everything in between. To speak up for yourself is to find yourself; insecurities shouldn't be held onto, as they'll grow as big as fear. That's why your purpose should be bigger than you. People would ask, "Why are you doing that? How come you believe it will take forever to go back to school?" I learned that you can be pregnant with a dream or vision for a long time, and it takes a push to start. If you're not ready for it, the dream or vision dies. But if you force the dream or purpose and have belief in yourself, along with a prayerful life, nothing is impossible. People used to tell me I was ugly, not strong, that I couldn't talk right—for over 25 years, these ideas were embedded in my mind. So, I had to change it. I looked in the mirror every day, reciting affirmations until I believed them. People used to tell me to get a backbone or find my confidence, but not too much because I might become an angry witch. How can I find a backbone when I don't have a blueprint? What is confidence when I don't see it around? Nothing is consistent around you, and what you thought was confidence is something entirely different from what you were told.

**Say it 25 times a day. See it 2 times a day (put it on a post where you can see it every day). Look in the mirror and read it until you start to believe what you say. There is power in the tongue (Proverb 18:20-21). From the fruit of their mouth, a person's**

---

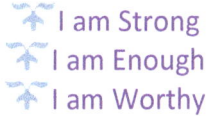

🕊 I am Strong
🕊 I am Enough
🕊 I am Worthy

stomach is filled; with the harvest of their lips, they are satisfied. The tongue has the power of life and death, and those who love it will eat its fruit.

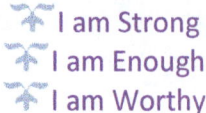

**Exercise:
List five to ten affirmations:**

I am_____

I am_____

I am_____

I am_____

I am_____

I am_____

I am_____

I am_____

I am_____

I am_____

---

🕊️ I am Strong
🕊️ I am Enough
🕊️ I am Worthy

You have to love every inch of your body, including its flaws. Understand that you are somebody and gain authority over your life. The way you were raised or hard life events does not define you, period. Listen to me clearly, everyone has a red wagon with rocks in it. As we grow up, we put 20 – 30 rocks into the wagon, some by incident and some we just picked up. I can only tell my truth, my path. By the time I was 16 years old, my wagon already had 50 rocks—too black, too skinny, body image, self-esteem, my speech, and the list goes on. These were the ones I put in my wagon. Then there were the ones my family put in: "You're going to be like your mom and dad—nothing. You're so dumb, you can't read well." Don't forget the rocks from teachers and friends that you let them put in. By now, your wagon is too heavy to push, and you can't throw them away, so I had to get another wagon. By the time I was a young adult, I stopped counting how many wagons I had.

Do not forget the generational rocks—those passed down by mistake from your mother or father because their parents passed them down. These rocks are heavy and hard to get rid of, like roaches that always try to come back or are hard to kill.

Realize that our parents raised their children the way their parents raised them. If their parents did not have the tools or knowledge, it means they didn't either.

---

🕊 I am Strong
🕊 I am Enough
🕊 I am Worthy

(Hint: if your parents only had screws to put up a picture, you will find other ways to hang it up.) So, if your grandparents only had screws and passed down only screws, that's all the tools you've got. But you know that you need a hammer. You don't know how to get the hammer because no one has the blueprint—we have to make it up as we go because we are all different; what works for me may not work for you. My path, my journey, is different. We may have similar stories, but they are never the same.

     Now, as a big kid, I love watching kids' movies with my children. In "Ralph Breaks the Internet," the character Vanellope von Schweetz had a glitch, and everybody thought she was the problem. They realized that she was the solution to the problem and a princess. It hit me that you should love everything about you, even the glitch; that's why you are unique. Ask yourself, do you stand in your own way? If so, does it interfere with your dreams, joy, or relationships because you're worried that you stand out for the wrong reasons or that no one would understand you?

---

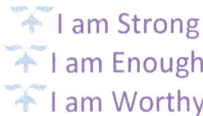 I am Strong
 I am Enough
 I am Worthy

# PHASE THREE
## Position your Heart and Real Digging

So, we've found who you are and embraced the process; next, let's check your heart. Unfortunately, people often don't know how to access their hearts because, at times, we're scared or we simply don't know how to listen. Instead, we live unconsciously, preoccupied with so many nebulous things. Guard your heart with all diligence, for out of it flows the issues of life. This means the secrets and solutions in your heart are your responsibility to guard, protect, and take care of (Ecclesiastes 3:11 NIV).

*Proverbs 20:5 says, "The purpose in the heart of a man is like deep water, but a man of understanding will draw it out"* (ESV). You must make time to quiet yourself and listen to your heart. Take notes on what your heart is saying. Ask the right questions and be open to the process. When you are not conscious, you may not know why you're drawn to certain causes, ideas, themes, or dreams. These drawings and dreams have everything to do with your heart, crying for you to stop, listen, and instruct you on how to fulfill, know, and understand who you are and live your life with purpose.

Children are so tuned in with their hearts; they are also free spirits until we, as adults, step on it. We, as

✟ I am Strong
✟ I am Enough
✟ I am Worthy

adults, have to be careful about what we put into and do to our children. God said to be childlike when it comes to Him.

Take two minutes and ask yourself: Do you remember when you were a child with dreams of becoming something (the sky was the limit)? Until when did adults say, "No, you're not" or "Why that?" Children don't see race, disability, or religion, only love.

 The second step we must take is deep diving. Water is a symbol of power, grace, and wisdom. It is also one of the four elements of life. Water can be related to purity and refreshment. Think about what water represents - a life-sustaining source. You are wasting precious time asking yourself whether you are good enough or if you want to hear yes or have people agree with you all the time (yes, people). Someone holds your hand every little step. You cannot bring everyone into your heart, which is your place of peace and joy. Please protect it. The book of Ephesians tells you who you are in Christ and has over 50 blessings that God promises you and me.

 So, when we start digging, we have to look at every area of our life—there are eight: emotional, social, financial, spiritual, mental, occupational, and physical.

---

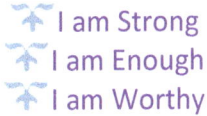

🕊 I am Strong
🕊 I am Enough
🕊 I am Worthy

Question time: **Who are you under pressure? Are you calm, worry, impulses etc.?**

_____

_____

_____

_____

_____

🌾 I am Strong
🌾 I am Enough
🌾 I am Worthy

**Do you know that pressure sometimes reveals impulsive decisions, and we make mistakes? Would you describe yourself as impulsive? Think of a time you did that and what the outcome was.**

_____

_____

_____

_____

**Exercise: Think about the best piece of constructive criticism you've ever been given.**

_____

_____

_____

🕊 I am Strong
🕊 I am Enough
🕊 I am Worthy

**How did it change you?**

_____

_____

_____

If we focus on our beliefs and faith, perhaps impulsive decisions will not be as prevalent. When life events hit us hard, we may go into overdrive—whether it strikes before, during, or after the fact. Do you work harder to avoid dealing with life events? You might work well under pressure, but what do you do if your personal life is under pressure? I have many stories that stand out, but I'll share two with different outcomes.

    I can remember a time when one of my children was shot. Yes, I freaked out; I called everyone I knew to vent and cry. I just wanted to get to my child. Time seemed to slow down for me, and my faith vanished. Every scenario raced through my mind. The hospital couldn't tell me anything over the phone. Impulse kicked in; for 48 hours, I believed nothing. My mind was everywhere because I wasn't there to see or talk to my child. I had to rely on other people, not my faith,

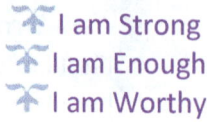

🌱 I am Strong
🌱 I am Enough
🌱 I am Worthy

and I made many bad choices at that time. These choices affected not just me but everyone around me. I was making decisions that even a child could have made for himself and me. I took away my child's power, and down the line, he was upset with me. I took away his voice and choice, something I fight against every day of my life because someone took that away from me. I did it to my own child with a snap of the finger. If I had just stopped, maybe the outcome would be a little different today.

Now, when my other child was in a bad car accident, I freaked out initially for about 10 minutes. But this time, I leaned on my faith, and I was not worried or distraught. I stayed focused on my faith, and people looked at me like, "Are you okay? Why aren't you doing anything?" The answer I gave was, "God did not tell me to move yet." Both of my children are okay, and both situations were under pressure but had different outcomes.

---

🕊 I am Strong
🕊 I am Enough
🕊 I am Worthy

## Exercise Four:

The circle in the center is your heart. Name your family and friends who are close and who are far away. Ask yourself why these people are closer than others. Now, after you do that, do your core values and morals match up with your heart? Again, ask the question of why they are so close to your heart or far from your heart.

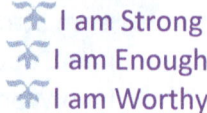

🕊 I am Strong
🕊 I am Enough
🕊 I am Worthy

# EXAMPLE

---

✈ I am Strong
✈ I am Enough
✈ I am Worthy

**Exercise Four:**
Fill in your heart below.

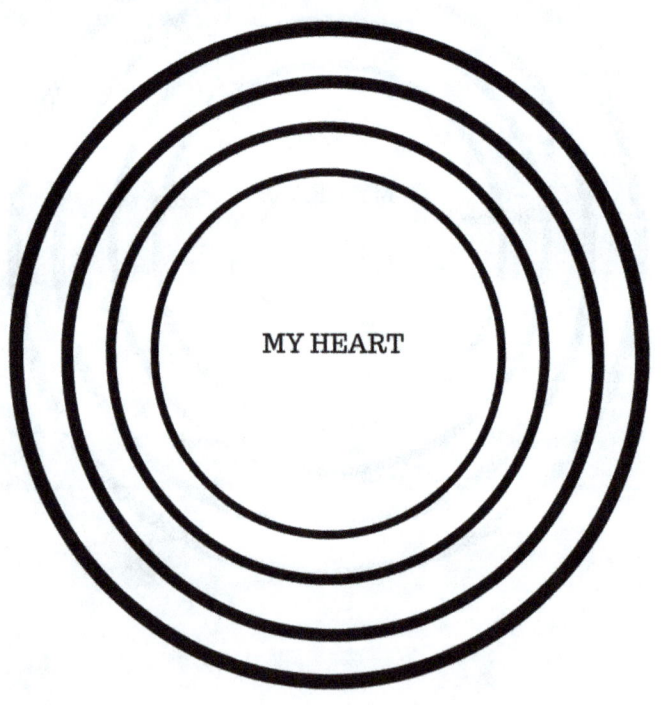

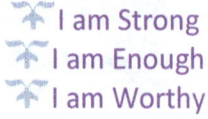 I am Strong
 I am Enough
 I am Worthy

Someone is dying, cannot invent something, cannot start their purpose because of you. There's never any one piece of yourself that you can give to a person without another part of you being involved. It can be a handshake, but it will certainly be your arm. This is about giving your heart without considering the part of it that beats, bleeds, and can be broken. So again, who are you; the real you?

_____

_____

_____

_____

Deep-water diving. When you dare to totally live, you position yourself to REFRESH, RENEW, and RESET your mind, as well as someone else's. Regardless of your wealth, success, or misfortune, if you work on bringing your purpose from the depth of the water to the surface, you must go diving and tap into places you must overcome. This means cutting it from the root. I had to forgive people that I really didn't want to. In my twenties, I forgave my rapist, my molester, my family

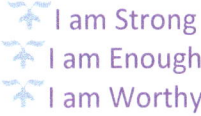
 ✦ I am Strong
 ✦ I am Enough
 ✦ I am Worthy

members who genuinely did not care or love me for me, family members that hurt my child, my parents, and the hardest of all, myself. If you're waiting on an apology, you will never heal from the situation. You may never get it, or you might get it years later. I learned that some people are toxic, whether they're family or not. You are allowed to walk away from a person and love them from a distance. I don't care who hurt you, family, such as parents, siblings, aunts, uncles, or friends. Allow yourself to create healthy boundaries. Please stop encouraging people to deal with toxicity and drama when they're not in a space to or because it's a respect thing. No, pray for them; let God handle their heart. You deal with your peace.

For me, my faith was always a strength of mine, but I did not understand how to use it or work it to the fullest. I recently understood my worth. I did the work throughout the years, but mostly, it was the bare minimum or just another thing that I thought was enough. Why? I did not know how to use the tools I had. We sometimes have the tools (advice) but don't know how or when to activate or pull them out. For me, it was my past and all the labels people put on me for years that when I thought I was done, I was not. I learned I was just picking the weeds when I should jackhammer, saw, chop to pieces, and then pull the roots out so it would never come back. My aha moment was when I stopped repeating the cycle of starting and

---

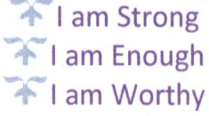

🕊 I am Strong
🕊 I am Enough
🕊 I am Worthy

stopping, and I finally rolled up my sleeves and did the work until I finished to the end. I was focused on God, and God was focused on me. We locked eyes, I gave Him my hand, and He led me with no questions asked. I started a relationship with Him. He was the parent (my Father), and I was the baby. God carried me when I needed Him to, fed me the Word when I was hungry, and protected me when Satan was coming for me. God gave me love when I needed to be loved, and God gave me a good talking to when I needed that.

Picture this: your heart has had an operation for years; you eat the wrong things, don't exercise, smoke, etc. You did not protect the heart. Now you have to protect it. The areas are eating habits (your past), smoking (forgiveness), and exercise (the labels).

---

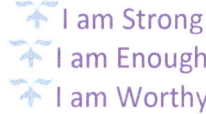

✦ I am Strong
✦ I am Enough
✦ I am Worthy

We must deal with all parts of the body to heal ourselves. **What are the areas you want to fix first?**

_____

_____

_____

_____

_____

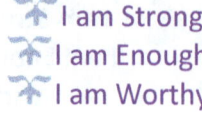

🕊 I am Strong
🕊 I am Enough
🕊 I am Worthy

## Exercise Five:

In the body, write how you see yourself; your values, personalities, and morals. Now, on the outside, write how other people see you, or things you hear them calling you? Why do they call you that name? (It's time to put a stop to it)? The reason I want you to do this is that sometimes we do things and don't know why we exhibit certain behaviors. If we acknowledge it, we are aware, and we can check it if/or when it happens. Remember, we are deep diving.

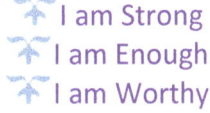

**EXERCISE FIVE**

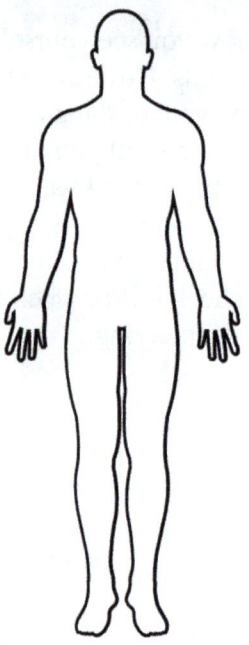

---

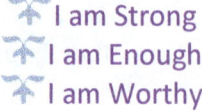
I am Strong
I am Enough
I am Worthy

# PHASE FOUR

## Embracing Yourself

The third step is understanding, becoming the person of understanding. So, we have an understanding of who we are, we embrace the process, check our hearts, bravely go deep, find the inner strength, and now, we need to understand. When you understand yourself, you can draw out the treasures that God has given you within. When you don't take a meeting, someone can draw your purpose out of you.

Note: If you're waiting for an apology from someone, you might be waiting for years (trust me, I'm still waiting). So, what I'm telling you is, healing comes first, and maybe the apology won't come. Don't wait for it; just surrender it. It's not going to make you whole. For this step, you might have to repeat it a couple of times.

My strength was sometimes my weakness. I questioned it many times. I have realized that God made me like this; He designed me from head to toe. I'm wonderfully made and transformed. He took my ashes and turned them into beauty (*Isaiah 61:3 - "To bestow on them a crown of beauty instead of ashes, the oil of joy instead of mourning, and a garment of praise instead of a spirit of despair")*. You might not see it

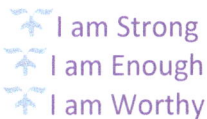

 🕊 I am Strong
 🕊 I am Enough
 🕊 I am Worthy

because you're in the storm, and when you're in it, you only see fog. Keep fighting your way out. Those stressors and labels have a hard hold on you.

**PERSISTENCE + HOPE + BELIEF = FAITH.**
Aha moment: I used to be mad at my mother at an early age. She made me write everything; I had to journal. If I was in trouble, I had to write a report on what I did and what my punishment would be. I had to read a book first if a movie or play came out based on the books. I had to see it and write the differences between them. She thought that since I could not speak correctly due to my speech impediment, my writing skills would be excellent. I hated it and did not understand it (we were in the storm). I had to find what worked for me so I could understand the lesson and it would stick.

---

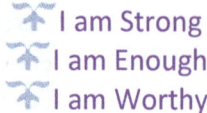 I am Strong
 I am Enough
 I am Worthy

## Exercise Six: Basic Cake Recipe

5 -eggs of faith
2 -cups of Compassion/grace
1-cup of kindness
3- cup love/wisdom
2 ½ -of forgiveness/understand
Pinch of patience
1 tsp of empathy
1tsp of character

*Faith* is the foundation, holding everything together. I must stand firm in what I believe and trust my Heavenly Father to guide my steps.

Just as I receive grace and mercy, I am called to extend the same to others. *Compassion* flows when we see others through the lens of love and understanding.

*Kindness* is a strength, not a weakness. It's a gift we give freely, expecting nothing in return, and a light in a world that often lacks it.

*Love* guides my actions, while wisdom helps me discern the right paths to walk. I had to learn to give a lot of love to myself. How can you say you love someone when you don't know how to love yourself? It begins with you. You also have to learn when to give

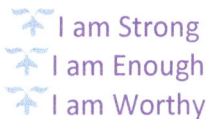

　✦ I am Strong
　✦ I am Enough
　✦ I am Worthy

love; everyone doesn't deserve your love. As I read more about love and wisdom, I had to pass it on to my community, the people around me. This wisdom is not meant to be kept to myself. It's important to plant seeds.

Forgiveness opens the door to healing, and understanding allows me to see beyond my perspective to embrace the hearts of others. I had to learn to forgive myself first, then I can work on forgiving the people that hurt me. I also realized that I can't and won't allow people to dictate my emotions or feelings. Understand that everyone learns at a different pace and goes through different things. Everyone needs a little bit of patience and empathy. Maintaining your morals and character is a must.

As time went on, I had to change my recipe; add a little more of patience, or less forgiveness. The good part is you can change your recipe as you grow. Have the ability to stretch yourself, your mind, and believe in yourself. You are like a rubber band, different is meant to stretch your comfort zone to be uncomfortable and believe you are not going to pop.

After a while, if you practice this you will remember this recipe.

---

🕊 I am Strong
🕊 I am Enough
🕊 I am Worthy

What does your recipe consist of? Does yours consist of understanding, confidence/ self-esteem? Write it down.

**YOUR RECIPE**

---

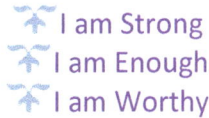
I am Strong
I am Enough
I am Worthy

You must truly believe that you can do it, even though it might take time. Once you understand it, stand in it for a while—this is your trust. Soak it in for a moment. This is the moment you realize, "I've got something here." For me, it's like hearing the song "All the Way Up" (Fat Joe and Remy Ma) in my head or "You Have to Encourage Yourself" (Donald Lawrence and Tri-City Singers). I realized that throughout the years, my strength or faith was not matched until it aligned because I did the work. When it happened, I faced the biggest fight of my life. It was like Ali vs. Tyson at 6:56 PM. They said who Cheryl was vs. what GOD said CHERYL was. I fought her many times in my life, and the old Cheryl always beat me down. I was not prepared, or I didn't understand what I was fighting for. You see, the Nay-Sayers were big bullies, but now they fear the new me, as I learn more about who I am, they get weaker. If you are now the real you, naked and all, and love and like every bit of YOU, anything is possible, and you are standing on your purpose. You are not afraid.

At the end of the day, we put the fear on ourselves. Sometimes, we are scared because we don't like change; we are comfortable, and we know what is coming because we've been there before. This step is crucial—you must forgive everyone and yourself totally. Sometimes, no questions asked, release every bad memory, thought, or someone's negative words

---

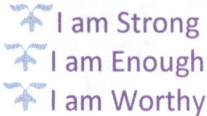

🕊 I am Strong
🕊 I am Enough
🕊 I am Worthy

spoken over you. You know the saying, "We can do 100,000 things well, but they will always remember that one bad thing."

---

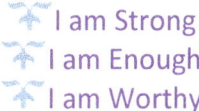 I am Strong
 I am Enough
 I am Worthy

# PHASE FIVE

## Don't Be Scared! Walk Forward and Rebirth

*"The theme you choose may change or simply elude you, but being your own story means you can always choose your tone. It also means that you can invent the language to say who you are and what you mean"*
**– Toni Morrison-**

After you cough up, spit out, and have a hard cry, knowing that everything is completely out, the real work begins. You must change. The operation was successful, but you need to change your habits. People may still look at you as if you've lost your mind or as the same old person. You need to celebrate and understand that you've overcome major surgery, and you won't go back to that place anymore.

Often, motivation isn't enough. Motivation is an emotion, and emotions are often fleeting and short-lived. While motivation is great for getting started, beware if you want it to be consistent. You'll need that

🕊 I am Strong
🕊 I am Enough
🕊 I am Worthy

willpower. I call willpower a muscle that can grow, but you must use it. With all things, I emphasize inner strength, deep diving, understanding, faith, and belief. By building good habits, your mind adapts to a routine, and now you are on the way to a life experience called Favor and Blessings.

When I journal, I always start at the beginning of my journal by envisioning what I will see in three months, nine months, and a year. It can look like becoming the employee of the month, starting a class, picking up a hobby, etc. In the middle of the book, I leave two pages to write down what I did and what would have happened if I didn't do it. At the end of my journal, I call it Celebration Time. I look at the beginning and middle of my journal, and there, I give myself a victory dance because I set and completed my goals.

My confidence and self-esteem were very low. It was so low that I had to dig deep to regain my confidence and self-esteem. I love music, so I created playlists, but I realized that one playlist won't do. I could not play it all the time because sometimes the songs would put me back in that dark space. So, I created several playlists for myself. I have about four: CeCe, Set in Stone, Just Do It, and Believe. These titles include R&B, gospel, motivation, and meditation. If I need a little push, I'm tired, I have to clean, or start a

---

🕊 I am Strong
🕊 I am Enough
🕊 I am Worthy

paper, I listen to Rocky's song (Eye of the Tiger) or Desiree (Gotta Be). If I want to meditate on God's Words, I listen to Kyle Lovett or the sound of rain. Remember, you can add or subtract songs as needed. I realized that as I started growing, I couldn't use the same songs anymore. I had to find other songs because the season had changed, and when the season changes, you change. Studies show that you should learn something about yourself every other month. So, what are you really telling you about yourself?

_____

_____

Your conversation with yourself should be truthful take off the mask. Is the conversation empowering? Are they affirming? Are you judgmental, critical, or maybe playing the victim? _____ Now look at what conversations you entertain the most. Are they bad or good? _____

---

🕊 I am Strong
🕊 I am Enough
🕊 I am Worthy

**Stop**: Go back and read what you say about yourself. Do you want to rewrite it?

What did you learn about YOU? Do you want to add more or subtract?

_____

_____

_____

_____

_____

🕊 I am Strong
🕊 I am Enough
🕊 I am Worthy

Sometimes, you must think outside of the box. We must declare and decree and become who we are. We pray for this and that – a baby, husband, or wife; a business, a home. We ask God for these things, but are we prepared to become these things? Are we walking into that season? If we desire to be a husband or wife, are we living as one? Are we faithful, supportive, caring? Can we shift from "I" to "TEAM"? If we're praying for a home, are we paying our rent on time, or are we still robbing Peter to pay Paul? Are we saving or just buying what we want, not what we need?

We ask for a lot, but we also need to prepare. We must get out of ourselves, stop trying to keep up with the Joneses. Who are they anyway? I haven't met them, but everyone seems to have heard about them. Remember, everyone has a season; find out what season you're in and why. It could be a season of gratitude, denial, acceptance, harvest, or forgiveness.

Everyone has glitches; some acknowledge them (True or False). But what happens when we know our glitches and release them too quickly? We must always check our hearts, deep dive into our emotions, understand them, and only then can we walk towards our goals.

Stay in your lane. Just because you're crawling and the next person is running doesn't mean you're not

---

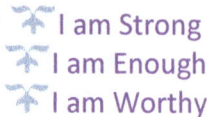

🕊 I am Strong
🕊 I am Enough
🕊 I am Worthy

making progress. We all have different math problems to solve (life events). You don't know how long others have been running – whether they're just starting, at 2 miles, 5 miles, 10 miles, or all their life.

At this point, ask yourself if you are hungry, angry, lonely, tired, or scared before you answer. Prepare for the journey with an open mind and heart. You have entered the HALTS stage. According to the dictionary, "halt" means to bring or come to an abrupt stop or a suspension of movement or activity, but the acronym stands for the basic internal triggers that sometimes result in relapse. Often used in addiction or stress management. Are you answering the right questions that frame your response in a manner that does not limit your possibilities?

---

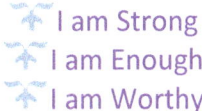
✼ I am Strong
✼ I am Enough
✼ I am Worthy

**Here is what I mean:**

| Prohibitive Questions | Propelling Questions |
|---|---|
| What good is this? | How can I use this? |
| Why is this happening to me? | Because of this, what will I be able to contribute to others? |
| Why can't I score in the top range | How can I better prepare to pass the test? |
| Why is my work and worth never recognized? | What can I do to make my work more recognizable? |

For years, people laughed and put me down about my speech—too squeaky, they said. I talk so funny, missing words or mispronouncing them. It's like my mind goes 85 miles an hour, but my tongue goes 145 miles—an inconsistency that never seems to catch up. Remember, I told you about the process. When God put me down, He really put me down to isolate me from everyone that and everything. I used to have bad migraines with all the side effects. I was working two jobs, dealing with depression, divorce, money because one of my jobs wasn't paying me, and trying to raise my children. Everyone was pulling me in different directions. People said they wanted the old me back.

---

🕊 I am Strong
🕊 I am Enough
🕊 I am Worthy

I had to rebirth Cheryl—the same person with a different mindset. This is my truth. I was never close to my grandmother, perhaps because of my mother's relationship with her. My father, from what I heard, was a great provider but not a great person overall. My grandmother treated me differently than my siblings, talking down to me, saying I'd be just like my mother—a waste with traits of my dead father. "You're not going to college talking like that. I told your mother to get your tongue clipped. You must get a trade or a job without talking." She mentioned other jobs I could do, but I'll let your mind wander on that.

My aunt told her to stop talking to me like that, and I respect her for it. I guess I held onto my aunt, and my children were closer to her than to my grandmother because I didn't want that negativity for my children. I realized that I was treated one way, and my children were treated a little differently. My godmother always played "Chocolate Girl" by The Whispers, "Ribbon in the Sky," and "Yesterday Me, Yesterday You" by Stevie Wonder. She planted seeds in me, and I didn't even know it.

My mother poured a lot of love into me—education, fairness, love, and forgiveness to all of us. Looking back now we had a different mother each one of us. She gave the best of her at the time. Now my siblings might say I had the best version my mother and

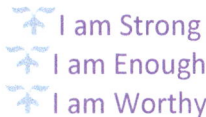
🕊 I am Strong
🕊 I am Enough
🕊 I am Worthy

that she was easy one me. I will say in certain areas, maybe she was, but my mother was dealing with addiction. When one couldn't, the other would. Funny, now I pour love out too. Both said, "You are love." After my mother passed, my godmother got hard on me. This was my second interaction with God. My first was when my father passed, I didn't want to go to school no one did. I smelled something but couldn't pinpoint it. The day of his funeral I saw an image rise to the sky with different colors; black, white, black, gray then white again. That day was strange, it was raining and sunny.

  When my mother passed, I saw an angel in my mother's hospital room waiting for all of us. My godmother asked me to go to the funeral home to privately say her goodbyes and she whispered in her ear and did her hair. At the end she asked my godmother to become my child(ren) grandma. She would tell stories about my mother and father. She would also speak life into me, "You're not a rug; stop letting people use you. Stop pleasing everyone; say no. You can do it; it will take time." As the old folks say, "Get a backbone; you don't have a gristle." My godmother planted the seed of "I never could've made it" by Marvin Sapp before he even wrote the song. She knew everything—my mistakes, my rights, my wrongs. She knew me before I knew myself. She's still in me, touching my skin, my voice, believing in me, encouraging me to follow my

---

🕊 I am Strong
🕊 I am Enough
🕊 I am Worthy

dreams and reminding me not to worry about the Joneses or the coulds and woulds. After my godmother's death, it was the hardest time of my life. She was the last person who truly loved, believed, and encouraged me. This is when I had to stand up on my two feet, not back down, get a backbone, and fight for me because I didn't have a net to fall back on.

So, I started the work. Sometimes I'd start, then stop, and start/stop. But I finally started and finished until I saw me for me. I started loving on myself more and more, believing in myself on a consistent basis, every inch of my body. I got naked, stood in front of a full mirror, and loved every part of myself until it was embedded in me. I am not what you say; I am what God says.

I am a child of God. I am enough. I am love. I am unique. I am ME. Some family members and so-called friends laughed and made fun of my speech. One time, a counselor in high school asked me about my plans after high school. I told him I wanted to go to a four-year college to play basketball and study design to own my business. This man told me I was dreaming and that with my grades (which were about 3.0), I should try vocational training due to my English grades. He always said that starting a business would be crazy in this day and age (this was in the '90s). Those words and what my family members said haunted me.

---

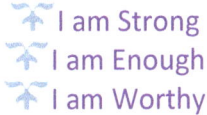
🕊 I am Strong
🕊 I am Enough
🕊 I am Worthy

I went to college seven times; I stopped and went every time a paper was due. Those words would come into my head until I had to reprogram my thoughts. Studies show that an average person has about 108,000 thoughts a day, and out of those 108,000, at least 70,000 are negative thoughts running through your mind.

Take a hard look at yourself in the mirror. What really holds you back? What are you afraid of? (Is that person you?) Pride and resistance to certainty have no place in this process. It doesn't matter how successful or unsuccessful others see it. It's who you're determined to create yourself to be and become.

---

🕊 I am Strong
🕊 I am Enough
🕊 I am Worthy

**Exercise Seven**:

What did you discover in your quiet room?
Are you speaking truth to power, or are you afraid?
How will you fulfill that purpose?

_____

_____

_____

_____

_____

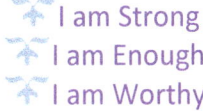

I am Strong
I am Enough
I am Worthy

So, I'm asking you, Who is
(NAME)_____?
Because if you don't find that person, the cure won't be found. Who will suffer because that teacher, doctor, or therapist is not there? We plant potential seeds in the ground so the crops can grow, but without careful, consistent attention and persistence, your harvest won't thrive. You must take a step of faith first in yourself before anyone will believe in you.

BELieve
In YOUR self.

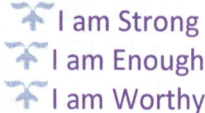
🌱 I am Strong
🌱 I am Enough
🌱 I am Worthy

*On this Date-*_____

*I (Name)_____,
will be present every time I walk into the room. I will not blame nor shame myself or others; I will build my confidence and self-esteem in myself by becoming my own coach, team, and cheerleader while building my support team. I will not look for it in a person, place, or thing. I will always respect myself and others. I will let the process work for me and be open as well as humble.*

_____
**Signature**

_____
**Witness**

*I attached a journal to this workbook. Start writing down your goals and dreams. Celebrate yourself and your accomplishments, big or small. This will be your receipt that you are doing what you envision.*

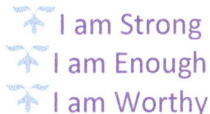

✈ I am Strong
✈ I am Enough
✈ I am Worthy

*Remember, who says you can't? YOU DO IT. Find your voice, trust your GUT, and GO for IT. This is your first step. IT starts with YOU and knowing who you are. So, when you can't see the work, or you want to quit, look at the journey to give you that push to go on.*

*Dear Current Self*_____

Here are some questions that might help to get you started (if you need it.)

Ask yourself those hard questions? Do you need something within your own happiness?

_____

🕊 I am Strong
🕊 I am Enough
🕊 I am Worthy

What goals do you want to accomplish for your family and your own personal goals?

Do you need to forgive yourself or/and others?

When you are alone are you content with being alone?

Do you completely love (write your name)

_____ in every area of life?
If you had a magic wand what is one thing you would change, and one thing you would keep the same? Why?

Be Honest with Yourself and Embrace the process to undercover a better version of YOU!

*Much "Wuv",*
*Cheryl Lynne*

## *Short Term Goals*

_____

_____

_____

🕊 I am Strong
🕊 I am Enough
🕊 I am Worthy

_____

_____

_____

_____

## Long Term Goals

_____

_____

_____

_____

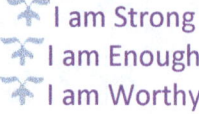

I am Strong
I am Enough
I am Worthy

_____

_____

# *"Your life is a message, find it."*

---

🕊 I am Strong
🕊 I am Enough
🕊 I am Worthy

*Stop!! Celebrate yourself and your small wins.
Write down some wins that you have experienced over the last few months.*

_____

_____

_____

_____

_____

🕊 I am Strong
🕊 I am Enough
🕊 I am Worthy

# "I am Unique"

*"I am Loved"*
  *Explore your Values, Needs and Wants*

**Values-**
*What is your definition of values?*

_____

_____

_____

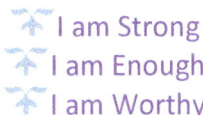
I am Strong
I am Enough
I am Worthy

*What are your own personal values?*

_____

_____

_____


*Needs-*

*What is your definition of needs?*

_____

_____

_____

*What are your own personal needs?*

🕊 I am Strong
🕊 I am Enough
🕊 I am Worthy

---

---

---

*Wants-*

*What is your definition of wants?*

---

---

---

*What are your own personal wants and desires?*

---

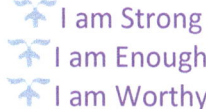

_____

_____

_____

_____

*"Wuv" Yourself*
*I AM RESILIENT*

🕊 I am Strong
🕊 I am Enough
🕊 I am Worthy

*"Get out of your head"*
*"It's OK to start over and try again"*

_____

_____

_____

_____

_____

_____

_____

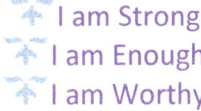

🕊 I am Strong
🕊 I am Enough
🕊 I am Worthy

## DON'T QUIT

_____

_____

_____

_____

_____

_____

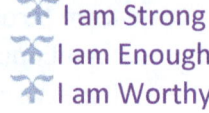
I am Strong
I am Enough
I am Worthy

*Today, I choose me*
*I am brave*

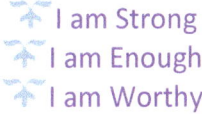
✈ I am Strong
✈ I am Enough
✈ I am Worthy

## *You are fearless*

*I am strong*

*I honor and respect myself*

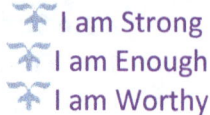
I am Strong
I am Enough
I am Worthy

_____

_____

_____

_____

_____

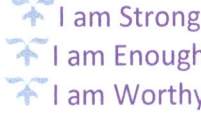

 🕊 I am Strong
 🕊 I am Enough
 🕊 I am Worthy

# *Guess what, you are doing it!*

*Take a look at your short term/long term goals.
Do you need to mark them as completed, or reset them?*

_____

_____

_____

_____

_____

🕊 I am Strong
🕊 I am Enough
🕊 I am Worthy

_I accept myself unconditionally
I am enough_

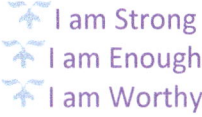
I am Strong
I am Enough
I am Worthy

*Short Term Goals*

_____

_____

_____

_____

_____

_____

🌾 I am Strong
🌾 I am Enough
🌾 I am Worthy

*Long Term Goals*

_____

_____

_____

_____

_____

_____

🕊 I am Strong
🕊 I am Enough
🕊 I am Worthy

*If you want to shine like a diamond, you've got to embrace the process.*

STOP!! Celebrate your small wins

---

🕊 I am Strong
🕊 I am Enough
🕊 I am Worthy

 I am Strong
 I am Enough
 I am Worthy

*Keep your face towards the sun and the shadows behind you.*

*I am strong*

_____

_____

_____

_____

_____

🕊 I am Strong
🕊 I am Enough
🕊 I am Worthy

_____

_____

_____

_____


*Believe in yourself and you will be UNSTOPPABLE*

_____

_____

_____

_____

_____

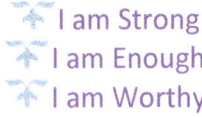

*Not everything that is faced can be changed, but nothing can be changed until it is faced.*

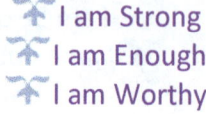
✈ I am Strong
✈ I am Enough
✈ I am Worthy

_____

_____

*"Be yourself, everyone else is already taken"*

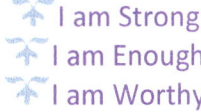 I am Strong
 I am Enough
 I am Worthy

*Don't Stop Believing*

_____

_____

_____

_____

_____

_____

_____

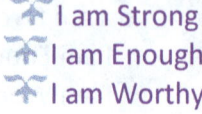
🕊 I am Strong
🕊 I am Enough
🕊 I am Worthy

*I will not worry about things that are out of my control.*

*My thoughts and feelings matter.*

---

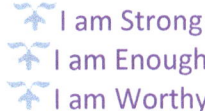 I am Strong
 I am Enough
 I am Worthy

_____

_____

_____

_____

_____

_____

_____

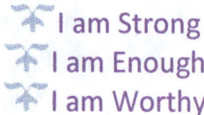
I am Strong
I am Enough
I am Worthy

*Do one thing every day
that scares you*

Who do you believe yourself to be?

_____

_____

_____

_____

_____

🕊 I am Strong
🕊 I am Enough
🕊 I am Worthy

*STOP!! Celebrate your small wins!*

🕊 I am Strong
🕊 I am Enough
🕊 I am Worthy

_____

_____

## *It's okay to REST!*

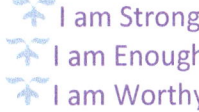
 I am Strong
 I am Enough
 I am Worthy

*Reflection Time*
*What did you learn about yourself?*

_____

_____

_____

_____

_____

_____

_____

🕊 I am Strong
🕊 I am Enough
🕊 I am Worthy

*What do you want to change?*

_____

_____

_____

_____

_____

_____

_____

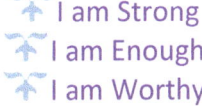

*How do you feel in this moment?*

_____

_____

_____

_____

_____

_____

🕊 I am Strong
🕊 I am Enough
🕊 I am Worthy

*The way to get started is to quit talking and start doing it.*

Patience is your power!

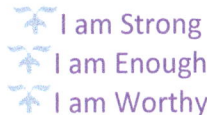
I am Strong
I am Enough
I am Worthy

_____

_____

_____

_____

_____


***Goals & Reflection***

*What is working?*

_____

_____

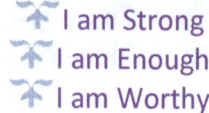
I am Strong
I am Enough
I am Worthy

---

*What did not work?*
*What can you change to meet your goal?*

---

---

---

*How are you going to move forward?*

---

---

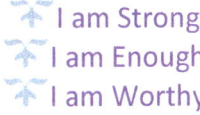
I am Strong
I am Enough
I am Worthy

_____

_____

_____

_____

_____

*STOP!! Celebration time!*
*Embrace yourself, look at. All your goals (small wins)*

_____

_____

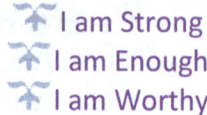
✈ I am Strong
✈ I am Enough
✈ I am Worthy

_____

_____

_____

_____

_____

*Never*
_____

    ✈ I am Strong
    ✈ I am Enough
    ✈ I am Worthy

# *Never Quit*

*Guess what, I believe in you!!*

_____

_____

_____

_____

🕊 I am Strong
🕊 I am Enough
🕊 I am Worthy

_____

_____

_____



*STOP!! Look at all your goals.
Celebrate your progress*

_____

_____

_____

_____

_____

_____

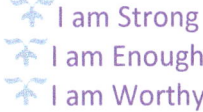

---

---


*Short Term Goals*

---

---

---

---

---

---

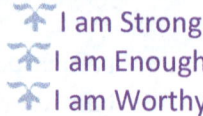
I am Strong
I am Enough
I am Worthy

*Long Term Goals*

_____

_____

_____

_____

_____

_____

_____

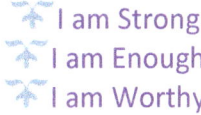
I am Strong
I am Enough
I am Worthy

*You did it! Look at all you did and celebrate yourself.
Embrace your hard work*

_____

_____

_____

_____

_____

_____

🌱 I am Strong
🌱 I am Enough
🌱 I am Worthy

## *About the Author*

Cheryl Lynne is, engaged to her love of her life, Aaron. She is also a mother of five and a Yaya to two. She

---

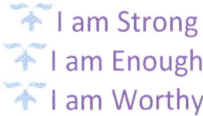 I am Strong
🕊 I am Enough
🕊 I am Worthy

overcome many diversities in her life that she dedicated her life to pour into hers and other children/families around her. Cheryl Lynne become a child advocate in the late 90's and community activist in 2010. As a relationship enhancement specialist (life coach) and natural nurturer who pour into people by educate, coaching using her life experience and trauma inform methods with uplifting the spirit.

    Cheryl Lynne Founder/CEO of Embrace With Wuv L.L.C in 2021 making butters, oils and crafting, speaking to young children to Embrace themselves the total self. She is a pray warrior, love to learn. She has a creative mind like to crocheting, sewing listen to all kinds of music. She equips families with the tools and understanding needs to motivate them. Cheryl Lynne works diligently and with integrity to ensure that families are not merely surviving but thriving.

---

🕊 I am Strong
🕊 I am Enough
🕊 I am Worthy

***Connect with the Author***

**Facebook:** Author Cheryl Lynne
**Website:** www.CherylsCorner.com
**Email:** embracewithwuv34@gmail.com

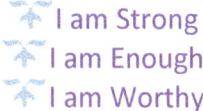

www.ingramcontent.com/pod-product-compliance
Lightning Source LLC
Chambersburg PA
CBHW060031180426
43196CB00044B/2371